SMALL FEATHER

poems by

Jade Rosina McCutcheon

Finishing Line Press
Georgetown, Kentucky

SMALL FEATHER

Copyright © 2020 by Jade Rosina McCutcheon
ISBN 978-1-64662-290-0 First Edition
All rights reserved under International and Pan-American Copyright Conventions. No part of this book may be reproduced in any manner whatsoever without written permission from the publisher, except in the case of brief quotations embodied in critical articles and reviews.

ACKNOWLEDGMENTS

This is my first poetry chapbook and I am so grateful to Finishing Line Press for picking up my manuscript, I'd like to thank Marc Janssen and all the poets in the Salem Poetry Project for your welcoming warmth and support and Eleanor Berry and the poets of the Mid Valley Poetry Society for your inspiration and support. Heartfelt thanks go to the Willamette Writers and for the honor of receiving second place in the Kay Snow Award for "Fair Art" (2019) and honorary mention for "Australian Bush Solstice" (2017). I particularly thank Paulann Petersen for teaching me how to bring imagery alive. Most of all I am grateful for each and every reader of this collection.

Publisher: Leah Maines
Editor: Christen Kincaid
Cover Art: Jade Rosina McCutcheon
Author Photo: Barbara Sellers-Young
Cover Design: Elizabeth Maines McCleavy

Order online: www.finishinglinepress.com
also available on amazon.com

Author inquiries and mail orders:
Finishing Line Press
P. O. Box 1626
Georgetown, Kentucky 40324
U. S. A.

Table of Contents

Australian Bush Solstice 1

A Stranger on a Platform 2

After 4

Agency 5

Below the Vine 7

Cuppa? 8

I Need You 9

Divine 10

Scrub 12

Beyond the Mist 13

Marble 14

Somewhere 15

Fair Art 17

Behind the Shed 18

The Interruption of Grief 19

Turquoise 20

Jelly Fat Slugs 22

A Forgotten Dream 24

Only Trees 25

The Silent Voice 26

Meds 27

Stella's Song 28

A View of the Horizon 30

Dinner Darling? 31

CRISIS 32

Journey into Green 33

Australian Bush Solstice

We party on the new pine deck
launch forth our summer joy
sautéed in garlic ginger echoes
bathed in Joni Mitchell's chords.

The bush is loud, hysterical
Kookaburras spilling riot-red laughter
silent kangaroos
grazing, listening.

Our revelry bounces off full moon light
flashes between stampeding clouds
as a summer storm excites the air
crackling the blue-green gums.

Party into jasmine-mango
barbequed prawns drinking yeasty
bubbles watching clockwork spiders
spin yarns.

Then a moment lily still
paparazzi moonlight catches us
faces uplifted
silhouette stenciled
into lavender summer night.

A Stranger on a Platform

She reeks of pale,
outer
planet starry stuff
sighing
dust and light
revolving
circumnavigating
late night
foreign
murky
trenches.

Shuffling blue sniffling
across the platform
wearing baby pink shoes
holy jeans
and an empty shirt
mindless
like she lives here
at the North Melbourne
train station
platform
an interstellar
guest.

Waiting for a
spirit beast
or a medicine woman
to follow the tracks
on her arm
make sense
of her life.

She leaves
finally
a small trail
of diamonds
following her
across the line
just as
a falling star
lights up
the sky.

After

Things stirring
strange
dead bird on
the lawn,
a blackbird,
who was my friend
and now, tonight
after you left
a small sparrow
dead
in the lounge
I am weeping outside,
under the stars
as though
the bird
were you
small feather
on the hardwood
floor
a sudden gust
and you're
gone.

Agency

I am creating
an advertisement
sharp and snappy
alluring pumpernickel
crunchy peanut chocolate
luxury lincoln car
kind of thing.

It starts with a huge
blue dirigible
floating very high
in the sky
with a see through floor.
Inside is a Dixieland jazz
some kind of
jellyroll morton
sweet georgia brown
kind of thing.

Hundreds of gigantic
orange elephants
run through
the streets
pink flamingos
on their backs
huge yellow lilies
in their
trunks.

A silver figure
then falls
from the sky
as the elephants
form
two letters
M.E. Me.
That is all
just me.
I want to be my
own advertising
agency
before there is no
room left.

Below the Vine

Tender bright green bunches
hanging on the vine,
it's what lies in the soil
that counts.

Old bodies
feed the grape
with all that once
danced
I've known you
through the weather
of fierce slippage
hard labor
with costly repairs
our friendship
fermented

you are gone
part of this soil.

Back to
green
tight bunches
hanging
in blistering sun
these hardy little
wine balls
remind me
what it takes
to make
good wine.

Cuppa ?

Instant please
ta
oh yes
an instant woman
gotta have it
when I want it
just an "add water"
kinda gal
gotta need
gotta fill it.

All that
planting, watering, nurturing , growing and reaping
is for the
farmers.

I'm hungry.

I Need You

I know you before I see you
cheeky rich musky grey possum
hurling brown nut macadamia tree
one thousand footed impossible centipede

I smell you before I see you
shy pink giggling daphne
seductive sweet rapturous wisteria
potent sunset red arid buck kangaroo

I feel you before I see you
silver light splayed across magical ocean mist
aquamarine too blue, too deep sea
naughty imp of wind tugging my soul

I hear you before I see you
gurgling musical maestro magpie
infuriating miniature annihilating mosquito
snorting old brickhouse wombat

Old healing tree
deep earth soaring hands
secret song catching arms
I see you
I need you.

Divine

I feel I have accomplished
high business
if I make it through
the week
with the washing done.

I am successful if I manage
to read
and pay all the bills in a week,
keep the kitchen bench clean
and keep food in the fridge.
I have achieved my highest aim
if I managed to make doctors,
dentists, hearing,
physio and Pilates appointments
for my mother
and actually attend those
on time.

If I manage to provide
a breakfast lunch and dinner each day
I am divine
if I manage to keep
my mother happy with purchases of clothes,
small gifts, soap, a trip to the movies
I am of angelic order.

I am a carer
full time
by myself
I often wonder how others
afford the time
to plot the demise of kings and queens.

Some days
I do not want to wake,
or get up, or shop,
or mow the lawn.

As she slowly loses her hold on her movie,
so do I on mine.
A slow death for us both….

Bless me, I have just finished filling the dishwasher.

Scrub

Smashing rain
belting the tips
off my memories
I scrub scrub scrub
the drops away.

I know she has to go
I know she must leave
(we all do)
as sure as the leaves
her time is coming
caretaker.

Each day her light
lit soul
is saying
'appreciate me,
I might not see
the morning light'.

It's cold
I dare not
close the window
for fear of
locking us both in.

Beyond the Mist

The mist limps
like a hobbit
across the tops
of glassy greedy ferns
into the thirsty
mossy
deep silence
and waterfalls.

Edges of the
green/gray river
are blurred by
sweet fog
merging with
foggy blue
light

and the deer
must be certain
where
she places
her tentative
hoof
for the ocean
lies
just beyond.

Marble

If I had but one marble
I would stare at it for hours
I would roll it and roll it
along every road
down every slope
around every curve
marveling at the way
the light hits
incandescent colors
as it rolls along
I would squeal with delight
just me and my marble

If I only had one thing
to see life through
to help me   weave time
into beautiful spaces
just being   so zen
just breathing   om
that marble would do
just nicely.

Somewhere

I lie down
on the soft grass
listening to the sounds
of children laughing
dogs barking
and drift back
to my childhood
when we would go
to the park
as a family
a time for us
to be together
as a family
but - not quite
my mother
never liked it at all
she was always
in the background
with a determined look
on her face.

It was hard
for women
back then
trying to
look good
hours spent
on makeup
heels, stockings
while my dad
and us kids
wore sneakers
shirts and shorts
ready to roll
in the grass
jump in a canoe
run and climb trees.

She would just sit
looking
somewhere
into the distance
deep blue
long ago.

I stretch out
under the tree
bare feet resting
on green grass
watching acorns
on the branch
little clusters
of great oak
my gaze
drifts
up through branches
in between spaces
drifting,
somewhere.

My mom on a picnic 1960s

Fair Art

A mysterious blanket
of falling white sails
and multi colored marbles
the art fair arrives
in hotentot orange heat
and settles like a peacock
feather on an emerald field.

Black raven, red cherry
ruby pearl flowers
on a blackwood maple box
stare back at her
jazzing and jiving
with their dizzying
collisions of mesmerizing colors.

For a moment
she hesitates
the current driving
her back
two shiny silver sticks
poking the air,
looking for purchase.

Head down,
she carries on
ambling gait on four legs
two flesh, two metal
going against the stream
making her own
way
like a brush
across the canvas.

Behind the Shed

Creaky breath
ten times she closed
the battered broken down door
opening and closing
again and again
willing the scene to be different
urging a new horizon
another sky
a different shade
another memory
behind the old shed
at the back
of the garden.

Squeaky handle
aches as it turns
stretching open
to red only red
the stream of her own
washed away
child.

The Interruption of Grief

There was a program
about memory
on the radio
something about it
took me away
into clouds
white puffy spaces
like cartoon balloons
always about to become
moments
interrupted
by the breeze.

I found a seat
overlooking
the view
from the vineyards
watching a memory
settle into the landscape
shuffling its feet
and laughing
like an elusive rope hanging
down the wall of a well
to the moment
of my grief
over you.

Turquoise

Deep, rich
turquoise blue
perches defiantly
on claret-red
impossible cliffs
vermillion flycatchers
sigh and preen
on either side
while the idiotic sound of
a musty ticking clock
creeps through the
old woman's home.

Carol King's *Tapestry*
sultry smoke
snaking heaven
emerald deep green
as old barnacled hands
reach once more
for the squid ink inkwell
and with an owl-like stare
at the delirious sky
she writes the
new moon
into her lonely
anemone-filled heart.

As she writes
a beetle nearby clicks
Rachmaninov
a narcissistic frog
chants a cosmic refrain
it learnt as a gypsy
in Madrid
her hands dance
past and beyond
the words

weaving
a madrigal circus of apricots
dressed as sirens
in the distance
and her mind dances
away on a typhoon.

Sun deep carmine
falls into dusty
orange light
sweet cumin
smells dance
spilling upon
all the life
in that house
coming together
deep inside
the violet scented
turquoise
heart.

Jelly Fat Slugs

It starts with the weavers
the sewers
the growers
moves on up
the chain to
distributers, marketers,
management, to the bankers,
the brokers, the investors,
and 'we' the people
can only gaze upwards
in awe
at the towering symbols
to wealth filched
ice-hard megalomania
to a place where the oversized
jellyfat slugs feed
on the top of the farmer's
sweat, the miners soot,
the laborers hard, daily grind.

Top feeder slugs
hardly move, like
a gigantic all-consuming
parasite
binding the mound
with a toxin binding the masses.

Brueghel's faces
trapped in
Dante's inferno
or Purgatorio
whichever way you want to look at it
but even Jabba the Hut
can't find Paradiso.

The local council member
taking the bribe
the banker making billions
my neighbor hating me
or the king developer
using all the town's resources
to make himself rich
leaving dying fish
flapping on the ground.

A Forgotten Dream

Salt the forever
into aching
winding chasms
weirdly walking
green talking
mouths about
a planet
you never even
heard of
a world with
the goal posts
so far apart
no point is left

forget me not
stars
on the loose
in the political caboose
the abyss
just up ahead
loose click clacks
the railway tracks
disappear
we carry on regardless
of the facts

like we didn't
notice the rails are gone
lost loons
in the light
of a full moon
stunned zombie
apocalypse.

Only Trees

I live in a sculpture,
covered in puzzles
listening to murmuring songs
below babbling brooks
talking with trees,
always trees,
only trees will listen.

I see three chickens
laying heads
instead of eggs
or are they?
I read words and hear songs
filtering sound
through fingertips,
I like to take long walks
along the soft afterglow of headlamps.

Beside me the trees just sigh,
beetles grind,
grasses explode
birds die laughing.
I'm no longer young
but does it matter?

This puzzle aches
for a serene and simple song
raw core orange
juice of the artery
between blue
green and violet
my day passes.

Blue jays chatter
family hysteria
I knit a daughter of the light
a child of the web,
this earth, the moon and stars
and so it goes, beyond description.

The Silent Voice

Grandmother Lil
was beaten to pulp
by Grandfather Bob
baby Pat watched
and when he grew older
he beat his wife Lulu
and his mother Lil watched
and his son Abel watched
and no-one cared.

Lulu went to court
to get a little help
for Pat was
breaking children's bones
the judge was
kind
but sent her
back
to live with Pat.
Her son is three
And so it goes.

Meds

The divine
is blue
sleeping
in traffic
drivers none
the wiser
the divine
is on meds
flowing
pharmaceuticals
through underground
rivers
stormy waters
no-one
notices
they
are no longer
moving.

Stella's Song

An empty song
hops along
a lonely potholed street
sad notes and totes
dead riverboats
searching for a beat.

A tune not far
by a long lost star
seizes the war torn song
a jive and a hop
a crackle and pop
the cha cha tags along.

A melody
so remote
hears the Latin beat
hops a train,
a bus, a star
and makes that song unique.

Stella, lady of the night
gathering galaxy dust
bag by bag
she sorts her goods
into piles
she calls her stuff.

That empty song
now so strong
fills her life-sore feet
old Stella dances
forgotten steps
seducing the moon
with that beat.

A passer by glanced
down the lane
hearing a moan of joy
but all he saw
was an old bag woman
holding a windup toy.

A View of the Horizon

Brown green earth stops
and blue begins
my breath deepens
I expand.

He often blotted out
the blue
when he was mad
blocked out the
light
locked in the earth
without breath
a terrible matter
the line separating earth from sky
is painfully thin.

We were sky children
With no earthly answer.

Dinner Darling ?

Chop, thwock,
wok crock thop
chutta chutta
whoomph whoomph
choppa choppa
thwack,
can the breadboard take it?

Sense blasting garlic, ginger, onion
into betty's frying pan, sizzle pop
watcha got ?

Purring wheezing fills the air
garam masala, cardamom coriander
betty's pan transmutes it all
into lava like
gangbusting elements
fistful smacking aromas
that whackydoo
the senses
mesmerize the mind
tornado the room
and smack my tired old being
into next year
oh yes, a little dinner
darling.

CRISIS

Guards like ants
at the edge of honey
work like beavers
or cattle dogs
to stem the tide
of this new river
snaking across
soul
breaking
deep old
boundaries
of laws and legends
forging new
tear trapped trails
ignoring where one
country, one people
one way of life stops
and another begins.

The force of this
roaring rapacious river
pushes aside
differences
your child is
my child
we are walking together
our life
on our backs
our hearts balloons
on tenuous string
as we weave
or way forward
searching desperately
with every bit of strength
we possess
for a place
to call home.

Into Green

A journey into green she goes,
she flies on deep within
upon the stream, within the dream
a holy oak she screams.

Whisper where you are
whisper where you be
she falls, she sits, she sits and thinks
beneath that great oak tree.

Over here, under there,
she flits, she mopes, she yearns
for frogs and birds that dance and sing,
she dreams to stay afloat.

Whisper where you are dear,
whisper where you be,
I've journey'd far into this wood
to hear you speak to me.

Up and down she ran, she sang
until she sank within,
deep inside that swirling stream
she wove her dream fog thin.

Is it just myself, myself I fear,
who sits by yonder tree?
or is it the girl who screamed a note
 to float upon the sea.

Whisper where you are now,
whisper where you be
I've journey'd long across this sand
to hear you sing to me.

She paused, then sang that note,
she sang it loud and strong
into the stream, out of the dream,
she answered: 'here I am'.

Within the stream
inside the dream
a holy oak she cried
a journey
took her deep within
the holy oak,
she fell, she died.

A journey ended, yet begun,
a spider's web is still being spun,
around, within, the frog still sings
inside the forest green, there spins…….

                                            a dream.

Australian born **Jade Rosina McCutcheon** holds a Doctor of Creative Arts from the University of Technology, Sydney and a Doctor of Philosophy from the University of Melbourne. She graduated from N.I.D.A. Sydney as a theatre director and has worked as a professional director in Australia and the United States as well as in many Universities. Her publications include books, *Awakening the Performing Body, Embodied Consciousness Performance Technologies, Narrative in Performance*, chapters in edited, peer reviewed volumes and poetry in Australian magazines. She was awarded second place in the Kay Snow Poetry Prize (Oregon) for her poem 'Fair Art' in 2019. She also has three poems published in *Terra Incognita* (Bob Hill publishing 2019). Jade lives in Salem, Oregon with her partner and their Australian Labradoodle.

www.ingramcontent.com/pod-product-compliance
Lightning Source LLC
LaVergne TN
LVHW041603070426
835507LV00011B/1288